THIS LAND CALLED AMERICA: **MICHIGAN**

CREATIVE EDUCATION

Published by Creative Education
P.O. Box 227, Mankato, Minnesota 56002
Creative Education is an imprint of The Creative Company
www.thecreativecompany.us

Book and cover design by Blue Design (www.bluedes.com)
Art direction by Rita Marshall
Printed in the United States of America

Photographs by Alamy (aaron peterson.net), Corbis (James L. Amos,
Bettmann, REBECCA COOK/Reuters, Richard Cummings, Images.
com, Layne Kennedy, NASA, Galen Rowell, Rykoff Collection), Getty
Images (Netterville Briggs, Frank Driggs, Melissa Farlow, Kean Collec-
tion, Keystone Features, Bill Pugliano, Andy Sacks, Three Lions, J. E.
Whitney/Hulton Archive)

Library of Congress Cataloging-in-Publication Data
Riggs, Kate.
Michigan / by Kate Riggs.
p. cm. — (This land called America)
Includes bibliographical references and index.
ISBN 978-1-58341-647-1
1. Michigan—Juvenile literature. I. Title. II. Series.
F566.3.R54 2008
977.4—dc22   2007019627

First Edition
9 8 7 6 5 4 3 2 1

This Land Called America

MICHIGAN

Kate Riggs

Michigan

KATE RIGGS

A GROUP OF PEOPLE BOARD A BUS NEAR DETROIT, MICHIGAN. THEY ARE NOT GOING TO WORK. THEY ARE ABOUT TO TOUR THE PLACE WHERE CAR MANUFACTURING WAS BORN. AT THE HENRY FORD MUSEUM IN DEARBORN, MICHIGAN, PEOPLE CAN LEARN ALL ABOUT THE HISTORY OF THE AUTOMOBILE. THEY CAN SEE THE LAST MODEL T CAR EVER MADE, THE FIRST MUSTANG, AND EVEN A CAR THAT HAS ALL ITS INTERNAL PARTS ON THE OUTSIDE! AS THE BUS TOURS THE GROUNDS OF FORD'S HISTORIC ROUGE FACTORY COMPLEX, VISITORS LEARN A LOT ABOUT CARS. THEY ALSO LEARN ABOUT THE RICH RESOURCES OF THE STATE THAT GAVE CARS TO AMERICA: MICHIGAN.

YEAR

1618 French fur trader Étienne Brulé becomes the first European to explore Michigan.

EVENT

Trade and Travel

FOUR HUNDRED YEARS AGO, AROUND 15,000 AMERICAN INDIANS LIVED IN THE AREA NOW KNOWN AS MICHIGAN. TRIBES SUCH AS THE CHIPPEWA LIVED IN NORTHERN MICHIGAN. THE MIAMI AND OTTAWA LIVED IN THE SOUTHERN PART. THE INDIANS FISHED IN THE CLEAR RIVERS. THEY TRAVELED OVER THE GREAT LAKES IN LARGE CANOES. THEY HUNTED ANIMALS SUCH AS ELK, DEER, AND BEARS IN THE FORESTS.

Chippewa chief

ne 1700s, the French
e into conflict
a American Indians
oosite) such as the
pewa (above)
ay times before
ing peace.

In the early 1600s, men from France discovered Michigan. They were eager to trade animal furs with the Indians and explore the large lakes. French explorer and priest Jacques Marquette founded the town of Sault Sainte Marie in 1668. Then French people had a place to stay in the new land.

The French were excited about living in the wild land of Michigan. There were many animals in the forests that they could trap. Then they could sell the furs and make money. In 1701, the French built Fort Pontchartrain where the city of Detroit now sits.

YEAR

1701 — Fort Pontchartrain is built on the site of the future city of Detroit.

EVENT

Later in the 1700s, people from England came to the area, too. They built a fort on Mackinac Island. It lies between the northern and southern peninsulas (landmasses surrounded by water) of Michigan. The English and French did not want to share Michigan, though.

The two countries fought over the land during the French and Indian War of 1754–1763. The English eventually won, but then they had to battle the American colonists in the Revolutionary War. When England lost that war in 1783, Michigan became a territory of the United States.

The Michigan Territory became important to the U.S. when the Erie Canal was built in 1825. The canal was a waterway that connected the East Coast to the Great Lakes. Now people and goods could travel much faster. On January 26, 1837, Michigan was made the 26th state in America.

In 1845, people started flocking to northern Michigan to mine for iron ore. The solid pieces of iron could be shipped to other states around the Great Lakes. Iron was not the only thing that ships carried in the mid-1800s. Many slaves from the southern U.S. escaped to Canada by traveling first to Michigan.

The issue of slavery helped start the American Civil War in 1861. Soldiers from Michigan were with the North and

At 363 miles (584 km) long, the Erie Canal was built in only seven short years.

YEAR

1760   The French surrender Fort Pontchartrain to the British, ending their control of Michigan.

EVENT

- *9* -

Jefferson Davis was captured in Georgia in May 1865 and was imprisoned for two years.

Fifteen millionth Ford

fought to end slavery. One group of Michigan soldiers captured the man who declared himself president of the South, Jefferson Davis, in 1865.

After the war ended that year, more people moved to Michigan and other areas in what is now the Midwest. The new settlers needed wood to build houses. In Michigan, many trees were cut down in the forests. By 1870, Michigan was producing more lumber than any other state.

In 1903, Henry Ford started the Ford Motor Company in the city of Detroit. Michigan was soon producing more cars than lumber. The state became known as the automobile capital of the world in the early 1900s.

People liked Ford's cars because the cars did not cost a lot. But in the 1940s, when the U.S. fought in World War II, Detroit's car factories stopped making cars and started making airplanes, ships, tanks, and other military equipment. Many of Michigan's largest companies continue to make car parts and develop new technology today.

YEAR

1783   Michigan becomes part of the U.S. after the Revolutionary War.

EVENT

The fifteen millionth car that the Ford Motor Company produced was its most famous kind, a Model T.

Lake Effects

Michigan's land is divided into two peninsulas, which are separated by Lake Michigan, the largest freshwater lake in the U.S. Lake Michigan forms the western border of the Lower Peninsula and part of the southern border of the Upper Peninsula.

Lake Michigan and three of the other Great Lakes (Huron, Superior, and Erie) surround Michigan's peninsulas on every other side except for their southern borders. To the south of the Lower Peninsula are the states of Indiana and Ohio. Part of the state of Wisconsin forms the Upper Peninsula's southern border.

Michigan's shoreline along the lakes is 3,288 miles (5,292 km) long. That is longer than any other inland state's. There are also more than 300 rivers in Michigan. All of the rivers flow into the Great Lakes. Important rivers in the Upper Peninsula include the Escanaba, Ontonagon, and Whitefish. In the Lower Peninsula, the Muskegon, Au Sable, and Kalamazoo are major waterways.

The lengthy shorelines of Michigan's islands, such as Mackinac (opposite), and along the Great Lakes (above) are easy to see from the air.

Slow-moving sheets of ice called glaciers formed the Great Lakes. Thousands of years ago, the huge, heavy glaciers made wide valleys in the land. Then the glaciers melted, filling the valleys with water. These valleys became the Great Lakes.

More than 100 kinds of fish live in Lake Michigan. They include lake sturgeon, brook trout, walleye, and lake herring. In Lake Huron, along Michigan's eastern side, smallmouth bass and northern pike are abundant. Many people in Michigan enjoy fishing in the big lakes.

YEAR
1805   The Michigan Territory is created, and former judge William Hull becomes governor.
EVENT

- 13 -

There are thick forests on the northern and western sides of Lake Michigan. On the eastern and western shores, there are huge sand dunes. A sand dune forms when the sand next to the water is pushed into large piles by the strong winds that blow off the lake. As the waves go in and out with the tides, they help shape the size of the dunes.

Sleeping Bear Dune is the highest sand dune in the world. It is located in Grand Traverse Bay off Lake Michigan. At Sleeping Bear Dunes National Lakeshore in the northwestern part of the Lower Peninsula, visitors can climb on the 465-foot (142 m) sand bluff.

Sleeping Bear Dunes National Lakeshore not only features the famous sand dunes near the shore (above), but it also includes forests of cedar, birch, and maple trees (opposite).

YEAR
1817   The first public university in the state, the University of Michigan, is established in Detroit.

Porcupine Mountains

In the western half of Michigan's Upper Peninsula is a region called the Superior Upland. It is a rocky, mountainous land that ranges from 600 to 2,000 feet (183–610 m) above sea level. This is where the Porcupine Mountains are located and iron and copper are mined.

The rest of the state is covered by the flat, rich soil of the Great Lakes Plains. Many people farm on the Great Lakes Plains. They grow wheat, vegetables, fruit, and corn. Southwestern Michigan is a perfect place to grow peach, cherry, apple, and plum orchards. Some people raise beef and dairy cattle, too. Others drill for oil and natural gas.

Temperatures in the Upper Peninsula are always cooler than those in the Lower Peninsula. There is a difference of about 10 °F (4 °C). Michigan gets about 30 inches (76 cm) of rain a year, and it gets a lot of snow in the winter. Some years, the Upper Peninsula gets more than 50 feet (15 m) of snow!

Trees on the rocky shores of Lake Superior have adapted to the windy conditions and little soil.

YEAR

1837   On January 26, Michigan is admitted as the 26th state in the union.

EVENT

Lives of Service

MICHIGAN'S FIRST SETTLERS WERE FARMERS AND FACTORY WORKERS. THEY CAME FROM EUROPE AND CANADA IN THE 1800S AND EARLY 1900S. PEOPLE STILL FARM AND WORK IN FACTORIES TODAY, BUT MANY MORE PEOPLE DO NOT. THEY WORK WITH COMPUTERS AND FOR HIGH-TECH COMPANIES INSTEAD. MICHIGAN RANKS FOURTH IN THE U.S. IN THE NUMBER OF PEOPLE WHO HAVE HIGH-TECH JOBS.

Many Michiganites work in service industries as well. Bankers, real estate agents, doctors, and repair people do not make things that people can see or touch. They help others by performing a service.

Ralph Bunche dedicated his life to helping people. Bunche was born in Detroit. He worked for the U.S. government during World War II. Then he served in the United Nations as a diplomat. He helped countries that were fighting each other find ways to get along. In 1950, he won the Nobel Peace Prize for his efforts at peacemaking.

While industries built Michigan's modern cities such as Detroit (above), farm products such as apples (opposite) fueled the health of rural communities.

Gerald Ford attended the University of Michigan in the 1930s, starring on the school's football team.

Another Michigan man who served people through politics was Gerald Ford. Ford grew up in Grand Rapids, Michigan. He began his career in politics as a state senator. In 1974, he became the 38th president of the U.S.

Michigan has produced more than political leaders, though. It is also known for its service in providing food to America. Fruits, vegetables, and grains from Michigan are made into many different foods. Then the foods are shipped from the Great Lakes to the rest of the country and the world.

W. K. Kellogg was a man from Battle Creek who sold brooms for a living. When he was in his 30s, he got tired of selling brooms. So he joined his brother John in inventing the first breakfast cereals made out of corn and wheat flakes. By the time W. K. Kellogg died in 1951, his cereals could be found in stores across the U.S.

Kellogg and Post cereals are still made in Battle Creek. Gerber baby food is made in Michigan, too. A man named Dan Gerber

YEAR
1847 | The state capital is moved from Detroit to Lansing to help develop western Michigan.
EVENT

Today, Kellogg's makes many breakfast foods in addition to the 24 cereals, such as Corn Flakes, it produces.

YEAR
1896   The first automobile in Michigan is seen in Detroit.
EVENT

- 21 -

*he city of Detroit
(opposite) has bustled
*ith the activities of
*ompanies such as Ford
(below) for more than
* century.*

started making it more than 80 years ago. People in Michigan continue to lead the country in food processing today.

From its days as the capital of the Michigan Territory in the early 1800s, Detroit has been Michigan's largest city. People move there to find jobs. They also come for the city's culture. Detroit built its first symphony hall in 1919 so that musicians could have a place to play concerts. It also has interactive museums such as the Henry Ford Museum in the suburb of Dearborn. There, people can learn about the history of industry in the state.

YEAR

1900   Ransom E. Olds of Lansing opens the country's first factory for making cars.

EVENT

O ne of Detroit's most famous citizens is singer Aretha Franklin. Franklin spent her childhood in Detroit developing her expressive voice. Known as the "Queen of Soul," she eventually won 19 Grammy awards. Franklin's career started in the late 1960s with such hits as "Respect." Franklin helped make Detroit famous for its brand of soul music, which was known as Motown.

Many different people live in Michigan today. About 14 percent of Michigan residents are African American. People from Asian and Hispanic backgrounds make up about six percent of the current population. Most of the rest are white. People in Michigan today live mostly in cities and towns rather than on farms.

At the Henry Ford Museum, visitors can literally step into history (opposite); at the Motown Historical Museum, they can listen to history-making singers such as Aretha Franklin (above).

YEAR	EVENT
1957	The Upper and Lower peninsulas are linked when the Mackinac Bridge is completed.

Michigan Tradition

THE FIRST U.S. STATE FAIR WAS HELD IN DETROIT. IN 1849, MICHIGAN SETTLERS DECIDED TO START AN ANNUAL FAIR. THEY WANTED TO GET TOGETHER TO CELEBRATE THEIR ACHIEVEMENTS. THEY ALSO WANTED TO SHARE CULTURAL TRADITIONS SUCH AS FOODS AND CLOTHING WITH THEIR NEIGHBORS. SO THEY BROUGHT THEIR PRIZE-WINNING FARM ANIMALS, FOODS, AND OTHER PRODUCTS TO THE STATE FAIR.

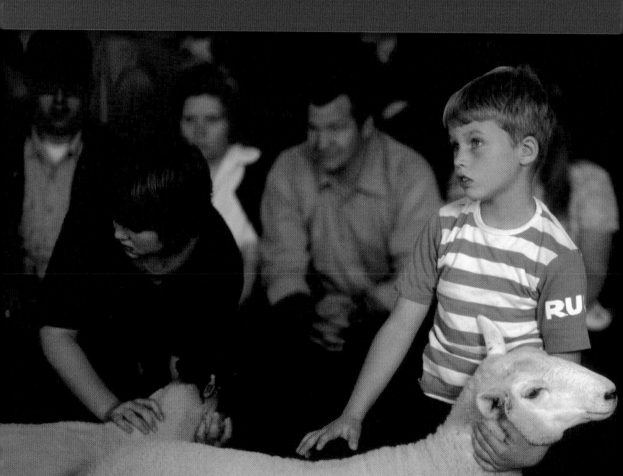

The fair was held in different Michigan cities for a while, but it returned to its present and original home of Detroit in 1947.

American winters during the late 1930s were some of the coldest in U.S. history. People across the country tried everything to stay warm. They even ordered red flannel underwear from a factory in Cedar Springs, Michigan. Since 1939, the small town north of Grand Rapids has hosted the Red Flannel Festival each fall.

In the spring, the town of Holland, Michigan, offers warm-weather fun. It hosts a weeklong Tulip Festival. In 1847, immigrants from the Netherlands settled the city in the southwestern corner of Michigan. They wanted to keep their native culture alive, so they began holding the Tulip Festival. At the festival, dancers wear traditional Dutch costumes and wooden shoes. People can see millions of beautiful tulips in full bloom.

The Michigan island of Isle Royale and the 200 smaller

While 4-H shows (opposite) are part of many fairs, Michigan also features unique cultural festivals such as Holland's tulip parade (above).

Comerica Park

Fishermen in the Upper Peninsula often wear high-fitting waterproof boots, or pants, known as waders.

islands surrounding it became a national park in 1931. It is the only island national park in the U.S. The park covers 842 square miles (2,181 sq km) of wilderness, harbors, lakes, and ponds. There are no roads on Isle Royale, only walking trails. People can reach it by boat or seaplane from the Upper Peninsula. It is 45 miles (72 km) from Michigan's Keweenaw Peninsula on the northwestern tip of the Upper Peninsula. That makes Isle Royale closer to Canada than to Michigan.

There are 500 permanent residents on Mackinac Island, but it, too, has remained largely untouched by time. People cannot drive cars on the island. All transportation is by foot or horse and buggy. Visitors can attend its popular annual Lilac Festival. Or they can step back in time at Fort Mackinac, the 18th-century British stronghold.

To reach Mackinac Island, people must first cross the Mackinac Bridge. Five miles (8 km) in length, the bridge spans the third-longest distance over open water of any bridge in the world. It is the longest suspension bridge in the Western Hemisphere. In 2007, Michigan celebrated the bridge's 50th anniversary.

Detroit, Michigan, is home to many professional sports teams. The Detroit Tigers have played baseball in the "Motor City" since 1901. Today, their home stadium is Comerica Park.

YEAR
1967   Growing tensions between whites and African Americans in Detroit result in five days of riots.
EVENT

The Detroit Tigers' stadium, Comerica Park, features a sculpture of a giant tiger as well as a mini theme park.

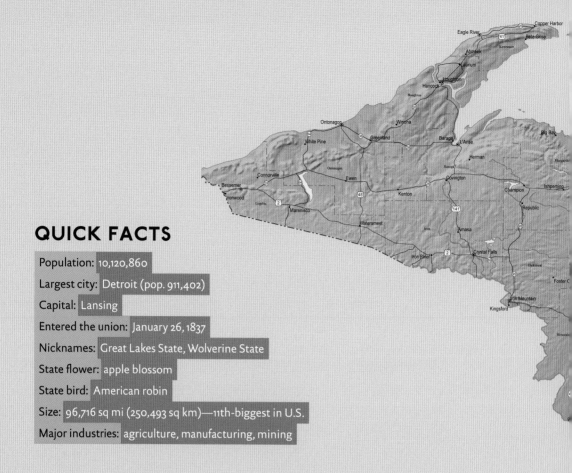

QUICK FACTS

Population: 10,120,860

Largest city: Detroit (pop. 911,402)

Capital: Lansing

Entered the union: January 26, 1837

Nicknames: Great Lakes State, Wolverine State

State flower: apple blossom

State bird: American robin

Size: 96,716 sq mi (250,493 sq km)—11th-biggest in U.S.

Major industries: agriculture, manufacturing, mining

The Detroit Lions are the state's pro football team, and the Detroit Pistons play basketball. The state's historic hockey team is the Detroit Red Wings, whose 10 Stanley Cups have earned it a reputation as one of the best teams in the National Hockey League.

From iron and copper to cars and tanks, apples and cereals to bridges and cities, the state of Michigan has produced many important things. People love to explore what it has to offer. Visitors travel to fish in its rivers. They come to boat on its lakes. They taste its foods and sample its history. And they always come back for more.

YEAR

2002   Jennifer Granholm is elected as Michigan's first female governor.

EVENT

BIBLIOGRAPHY

Aylesworth, Thomas G., and Virginia L. Aylesworth. *Eastern Great Lakes: Indiana, Michigan, Ohio.* New York: Chelsea House Publishers, 1988.

The Henry Ford. "Henry Ford Museum." http://www.thehenryford.org.

Kalbacken, Joan. *Isle Royale National Park.* New York: Children's Press, 1996.

Thompson, Kathleen. *Michigan.* Austin, Texas: Steck-Vaughn Company, 1996.

Ylvisaker, Anne. *Lake Huron.* Mankato, Minn.: Capstone Press, 2004.

Ylvisaker, Anne. *Lake Michigan.* Mankato, Minn.: Capstone Press, 2004.

INDEX